„Whoever is ascending towards
the light of truth
Must forget about himself
and dissolve the lie."

Andrea Regina Katharina InEssenz

edition inessenz

Andrea *Regina Katharina* InEssenz

Royal Road

Where are you?

Guidance for Ascension

Royal Road - Where are you?
1st edition 2021
by Andrea Regina Katharina InEssenz
www.andrea-inessenz.de
(Original Title: Königsweg – Wo bist du?)
Translated from German by Vincenzo Benestante

Editor / Author:	Andrea InEssenz
Cover design, typesetting & layout:	Roland H-P Lutz
ISBN 978-3-949324-01-7 (Paperback)	
Credit:	
Cover picture, pages 93, 102 & back cover	Roland H-P Lutz
Picture page 64 (Photo)	Roland H-P Lutz
Picture page 80	Tumisu
References: page 5 from	Bürger-Verlag,
„Ephides" - A poet of the transcendent	D-Hardthausen

On the author's website you will find more current, especially mystical texts. Visit for this:
www.andrea-inessenz.de or follow her on:
facebook: / Andreainessenz
twitter: / Andreainessenz
vimeo: / andreainessenz
youtube: // Andrea InEssenz

Royal Road

Where are you?

Guidance for Ascension

edition inessenz

„**Y**ou, generation, lost in turbid times,

Behold – black riders on the horizon!

Still shadowy, yet closing in,

The savage warriors of darkness are encircling!

Indeed, you've welcomed darkness often,

A shelter for your deeds to ripen,

And gladly did you listen to its whispering.

Behold – your deed's seeds are sprouting now!

Why are you shivering, unable to endure?

You were courageous once, when challenges occurred!

But darkness, once obliging to your goals,

Is now unveiled – behold its true form!

And sense the feverish tremors of old Earth,

And watch the house of science trembling,

And watch mankind's most holy wares plummeting down,

Entraining your best powers!

For suddenly, darkness is everywhere,

Turning against you, devastating.

Those black riders on the horizon are

The very evil you sent out once.

Yet, there is grace, allowing you to face the darkness,

So you can know it, and thus, knowing, be redeemed.

Therefore, boldly lift love's banner high against it,

So that you, while redeeming, may rise up yourself!

For you've arrived, lost generation,

At the abrupt end of your turbid road.

So, fall back into yourself, draw strength within,

And cause the great transition of this world's age!"

From „Ephides" – a poet of transcendence

Contents

Table of Contents

Acknowledgements   9

Foreword – „For your understanding ...“   11

Ascension or Descent   13

What is Mankind seeking?   23

The True Awakening   31

The Crown of Creation   39

Separation from the Light   47

The Erroneous Paths of Personal Empowerment   53

Occult Training   57

The Holy Power of Healing – Healing Magnetism   65

It is opened   69

The Adjustment to True Peace   75

Further Guidelines   81

Prophecies of Seers – Possible Fulfillment   85

The Essence of all Words   89

The Ascent to Mount Carmel   94

Afterword   97

    103

About the Author   104

Encounters with Andrea Regina Katharina   106

Acknowledgements

Once, I was a person unaware of myself, committing the errors of life and using my mind as a tool. A person who was often lost, hurt others, and was hurt. A person longing to be a mother and a wife, but still often failing in thoughts, words and deeds – a husk filled with emotions and thought forms, searching for truth and peace.

I THANK this life, as hard and perplexing as it was, with everything I am sanctioned to be. It taught me what a human being shouldn't be like, and its teachings were profound, leading me into a complete separation from God, and into the characteristic dynamics of human beings. It revealed to me how lost man is without the proximity of God.

I thank all those people who endured with me, and I ask them all for forgiveness … may they find their way back, as I did. That's what I was like as a human being without God, our Creator.

So, my heartfelt thanks are due to the divine power ... the Father, his Son Jesus Christ, and the Holy Spirit. As a person, my thanks also go to my soul, who never gave up, steadily leading me on towards home (into my true homeland).

Furthermore, I thank all those people in my vicinity who are also becoming aware, devotedly focussing more and more on the great transition.

Today, I am as God has lovingly formed me – intimately connected and united with the truth, freed of errors and temptations.

I thank the divine fiery power within me, which dissolves every veil and empowered my brothers and sisters to blossom as well, in the fire of spiritual love.

May the spirit of mankind be ennobled for a life in peace ...

May all of you be a blessed force.

Foreword

„For your comprehension ...“

Once the veil falls, faith can be experienced directly, becoming the only conviction. Here, complete liberation and peace are found, and man is redeemed.

This text was given for everyone, for the non-believers, (but also) for the churchgoers, and for all spiritual seekers and those who practise spirituality.

These words may be arousing, or cause outrage. Only those who have already opened sparks of truth within themselves will grasp the message, as in a reverie, and employ it for righteous actions. For those, this text might become a beacon. It is a summary of the essential nature of the human being, and of our Creator, God. It is unswervingly straightforward. Once discerned, it leads out of the dramas. In few words, it points out what the human being is, and what we believe it to be.

This script helps to realise that the natural movement of the true spirit is led astray by assistive devices and predetermined paths.

The truth of these words awakens the human being's abilities, which can then be employed, like a hero would employ them, whenever temptations and their consequences attempt to cross our path. While we are learning to own these words as our personal truth, the path of ascension is permeated by God's Light, and we can finally become free.

Thus, I urge all those who are AWAKENED: wake up and don't tire of examining your convictions. Become living humans and awaken from the sleep of death.

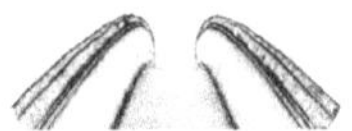

Ascension or Descent

Man is entwined in the web of his own snares. Let it be said here: don't become entangled in those webs, but free yourselves and become discerning in the light of truth and eternity.

There is an eternal law which caused the human spirit to create a body, which has become its home for many centuries – the causal body, or the causal kingdom. This originates from the law: „What you sow, you shall also reap".

Everything we human beings burden ourselves with, by thoughts, words and deeds, is our seed, weighing us down; however, we are the harvest as well, and therefore the redeemer of all those causal constructs.

Here, God's Righteousness is predefining the path a person has to follow in order to free his/her entrapped spirit, and lead it back into the realms of truth.

So now, we human beings are supposed to free ourselves! This can be achieved only by the solemn and genuine determination to enter into God's Kingdom. Here, honest and serious prayers, and the quest to be a better spirit, bring forth REDEMPTION.

It is not enough to have this intention and then follow it up with spurious deeds that resemble a compromise. Because the ignoble is tough, it binds and impedes. It pulls the spirit down and is like a magnet. Thus, dubious and dishonest intentions will draw the pre-existing ignoble instantly, and nourish it again, thus effecting a causal chain, like a rosary, whose beads are constantly repeating and complementing themselves – but the rosary is uplifting, and in this example, the causal chain is degrading.

If a human being renews him-/herself only half-heartedly, he or she can never rise up and ascend. Half-truths are no truths at all. And the law of seed and harvest can only be terminated by perfection. There is also the even greater danger of the spirit plummeting still deeper, to be captured by the ignoble.

Quite a lot of people are currently on the supposed path of „ascension", and their methods lead them to believe that they are already in the beyond, in the realms of ascension and redemption. They don't realise that large parts of themselves are only repeating everything in the causal body, while only one part of them is moving on.

Sending one's spirit into the spheres to gain messages and insights is no ascension. It always is a further illusion and disorientation, even though many people refresh themselves by it and feel good about it.

There is but one road to the ascension into the light, and that is the steady removal of false concepts and bad virtues. Without the firm will to „become the good", the quest to dissolve all misconducts and false beliefs can't lead to liberation.

Yet, whoever chooses to follow this path diligently can rest assured that he/she will be detached from the causal body with its repetitions, from the chain of entanglements and misdeeds. By the very purpose to become GOOD, we will lay down a rock of faith, which will carry us down all of the paths we need to travel now, on the way to liberation. Whatever we may now encounter, even losses and loneliness, serves exclusively to bring about our salvation, acting as a curative for our spirit, soul and body.

Can you, oh man, discern what your task should be? Can you grasp the value of this message, and make it your own?

I tell you and advise you to take this task on wholeheartedly, with everything you are. It encompasses harbouring pure thoughts, uttering good words, and doing helpful deeds. I advise you to never cease pressing on, applying all your energy and mental power. Thus, you change yourself and your surroundings.

And while you are endeavouring, perhaps seemingly making less progress than those contemporaries who talk to so called „angels" and „ascended masters", know this: your life is but a brief moment – you are dying and living in perpetual transition, and even when you leave the earth, you are who you are.

Isn't it an obvious task to transform yourself and grow up into the truth?

Growth is subject to the divine law of nature. It can't and shouldn't be rushed, lest you are hurt, or hurt others. Actually, your earthly body (the physical body) is shrouding your factual spiritual truth like a rampart, and without this body, many souls will be astonished and shocked by their true character. This earthly body will not dissolve in just any sphere, but only in the very same sphere its spirit is carrying. Therefore, it can hardly detect any light in its surroundings, which makes it twice as hard to disentangle itself from this distress.

Thus, it can be truthfully said that an ascension in the light, and towards the light, is much easier while in physical form, than whilst spirit and soul lack the sheltering bodies.

In the realm of Earth, in the earthly school, we can discern what is „good" and what is „evil" by our senses, which we receive as a human being on Earth, and by the free will. Here, „good" and „evil" walk the same road, and we must, on our way towards the light and towards goodness, walk through the „un-light" (evil) and infuse it with light (goodness).

Thus, it is essential to let go of the follies derived by our own will, and face one's true nature. It is not possible to make enormous progress, because no one knows how long his/her causal chain is, and how much time it will take to work it off. And therefore, we should drop the desire for a quick redemption and devote all our energy exclusively to a good, honest ascension.

Before a human being can spiritually rise up into the spheres, the old must be rebalanced – THIS is true for all mankind.

Don't loose heart if everything proves to be arduous and tough. It is not important to achieve success, it is not important to gain knowledge – it is only important to begin, and to discern vigilantly the bad, and to dissolve it slowly, but steadily. Thus, the karma chain will become shorter, link by link, and we can ascend joyfully and easily into the light of all eternal bliss. We will be free and embody peace.

Humankind has created a huge wall, a mountain of bricks and rocks, by wrongful thinking and wrongful deeds. When we choose the honest way, which is really the ONLY WAY, the stones will not be removed for us one by one. No, not so, for it is the wall of our own seeds, after all, and thus, every stone must be recognised and transformed in our consciousness, until the wall is levelled. This is also the explanation for the fact that so much suffering is manifested on the path of purification. All that which was suppressed and is now being revealed is inherently, peculiarly our own.

During this process, which at first seems laborious, the human being who is diligently walking this path of purification will soon realise full of awe that he/she is now accompanied by a deep love, which will manifest itself in all areas, and infuse itself into all the now cognisant rocks, transforming the rigid matter into light.

This is God, who is now dissolving the chains, and disentangling the knots alongside us, leading us with tender power to scrutinize everything, and thus, return everything to the good powers. Withal, God is as gentle towards us as towards a newborn child, which still needs its mother's all-inclusive care.

However, while working on dismantling a wall and a long causal chain, we need to muster a great deal of patience to endure this process. Because once a misdeed has been dissolved, the next one is already approaching, demanding the same procedure of transformation all over again.

Yet, as these processes progress, the human being will also experience an increase of love, and thus the stumbling beginning is now becoming a flow – after all, we are dealing with the Source of Love itself, which has now created a river.

That's because the ignoble weighs the spirit down, while the good relieves it, allowing it to ascend – such is the eternal law. It was Jesus who brought this enormous and sole teaching to earth. This is what he told every human being: „Love your neighbour as you love yourself".

That's the very gateway to the ascension into light. Because if a human being develops good characteristics and labours on behalf of creation, he/

she is sowing good seeds and shall reap good fruit.
„It is by their fruit that you shall recognise them“
– this, too, was conveyed to all mankind by Jesus.

To give ONESELF without expecting anything
in return; to give one‘s own self to our neighbour
– that means being able to LOVE as Jesus did.

The „good“ must help to remove the gradation
between human beings: „Go and feed the poor in
spirit – give them the food which is love“. Thereby,
radiating beams are reflected, which are entering
into your spirits and shall lift you up into God‘s
realm.

And to all people who are now asking what
is gained when the old breaks away, and what is
gained if we give ourselves over to goodness without
receiving anything visible in return, it should be said:
whoever frees him-/herself from the chains of one‘s
own power and one‘s own snares, and thus returns
into God‘s Realm, receives the highest reward, which
can‘t be found in this world of sin. Also, those people
should know: even if they free themselves, they are
still eternally urged to follow the Savior, and unwa-
veringly be the good – so be it.

„Whatever wishes to ascend,
must lighten itself.
Only by detachment and release
can both the spirit
and the soul rise up.“

Andrea Regina Katharina InEssenz

What is Mankind seeking?

With craving vehemence, mankind is on its way to ascend to the next level. This is every single man's deepest desire. Insights of the cognitive sciences are distributed in ever increasing numbers, and permanently repeated in new wrappings. It has become such a circus, and there are so many spiritual attractions, that the result for many seekers is spiritual exhaustion. From all nooks and crannies, as if multiplied by a virus, people pop up and offer „light"...

This spiritual fun fair tortures the human soul, which is already dysfunctional, tremendously. It is neither nourished by it, nor enabled to rise up. It is like a ball in a soccer field. It is kicked this way and that, constantly being urged to define itself in a new way as the SOMETHING it has always been. But all those words being whispered to it do not help it to comprehend how and what it is supposed to deliver. Our spirit is filled with too much chaos, and all the symbols the soul is supposed to absorb are only confusing it more and more.

For so many centuries, and even much, much longer, during the entire time of mortality; confusion, ruin and timidity are found in the human soul. It is searching for the ONE and receives so many attractants that it finally withdraws in exhaustion, sending energies of fatigue into the human body. In the past, the soul has received powers to such an extent that they were blighted by their own light, and thus, its goal and only task is to free itself from the resulting bog again and again. But the bog in the „swamp-life" of the soul is tough and does not allow for much movement.

The human seeker's cry for light and redemption has steadily been nipped in the bud – before the liberating deed could be accomplished, the commenced path had already been cut short, in favour of a new, preferably easier road.

And so, the human soul was never able to really leave its bog behind. What should we do differently now? After all, the actual influx is the same it has always been – the light, which the soul is yet unable to recognise. And this is supposed to bring salvation? Bravely, the human soul is attempting to open itself up to it.

Just look at everything offered … who can still discern what is right and what is fake? Everybody talks with the tongues of angels and styles him-/herself as a divine messenger.

That way, people are fettered and assured that the beyond is a safe and benevolent place. However, the concurrent dangers are not revealed to the seeker. For the beyond is the invisible place, co-created by the human spirit. How can the human being be sure that the light he/she is obtaining by means of all those offers is pure?

The same is true of all the texts which supposedly bring nourishing bread to those hungry for the light. How could a simple spirit enter into the state of insight with their help? After all, those texts attempt to clothe the „high" in words, while forgetting that the „high" has no words. Thus, one book after another passes through a person's spirit, and diligently and dutifully he/she tracks anything that seems to make sense. Some of it may be nourishing and refreshing, but a lot of it is stony food for the spirit, which recognises itself as still being in bondage.

Man seeks the fragrance of redemption, to dispel the reek of his festering wounds, which we often recognise much too late; for example when encountering cancer or any other ruinous cellular diseases. Then we start to understand those books we already read and realise that it is not the fragrance of religious ecstasy which is important, but the confronting of the shadows, so perfectly camouflaged within the so-called ego. Often, the seeker might even be a peaceful warrior, unaware of all that is still seething inside him/her, and of what may still be redeemed.

And then, there are so many people who had so-called „kundalini-experiences". They undergo out-of-body-experiences and mystical experiences which can't be put into words. And the way most of these people handle these experiences points out how addicted to the fragrances and the temptations and the proofs for its existence the ego really is. Because everyone who even once had a kundalini-experience has in the same instant lost his/her humility towards it. He/she wants much more of it, wants to repeat it, again and again, because finally, it makes him/her feel special. What these people can't understand and grasp, is that all these experiences are not special at all – they are just experiences, plain and simple. Most people who had kundalini-experiences are still twisted and are becoming even more confused, because now they walk in two worlds – one foot in the mystical, the other foot in the ego, which is always egging the seeker on to produce new adventures.

What no seeker is conveyed as knowledge and wisdom is, that the spiritual journey is always a path of loss, of bereavement, and of helplessness. Because in the end, it is all about loosing everything, without compromises. This journey hurts, because it is the injuries which constitute a seeker. Whoever is really allowing him-/herself to become spiritualised, will not gain anything. All his/her experiences are hollow, containing fears and utter nakedness, full of horrors and tears.

A real experience is like death – it disintegrates the very experience itself; it actually kills itself, because it doesn't include the scale, but the result does.

All the human being does on the so-called „spiritual" path, is to hoard a lot of mystical experiences and messages from psychics and healers for his/her own ego. After all, it is not expedient to use even one uncomfortable word in his/her presence, lest the seeker loses courage – the ego can't stand any advice or admonitions which are contrary to its own concepts.

So, again, the path of ascension is more about the ascension of the ego. Where, at this point, does mankind truly crave to enter into God's Realm?

Words and terms such as enlightenment, kundalini, light, messages from angels, channelling, contacts with the beyond and many more, are the language of the „spiritual scene". While talking about consciousness and light, hardly anyone in this scene speaks about God, his Son Jesus or the Holy Spirit, who communicates the Will of God. Almost every seeker is exclusively looking for the experience, and for joy and abundance.

Yes, the Heavenly Father wants his children to be happy. It is his wish that man may be content and joyful. This can't be experienced – it might, however, be earned, to restore the natural status of peace, which isn't like a drug.

**„Whoever opens a door,
has to be brave
to enter through it,
without a clue
about what's on the other side.**

**Thus, he/she is ready for
everything that is."**

Andrea Regina Katharina InEssenz

The True Awakening

Beware of your deeds and thoughts.

Awakening is an individual act – it can't be executed collectively. Because something which is good for one person may include a burden for others. We human beings all carry our personal road to perfection within ourselves – our gait, our very way of being. It has been invested inside us (in the soul), and there it has stayed, untouched. Solely the paths of the centuries have separated the human being from this natural potential.

The base for a so called spiritual awakening is the recognition of the burden, which weighs heavily on the human spirit, and is passed on to the physical body.

All true bondages of the human being, all the chains, all the burdens, reside inside our own spirit. Thus, it may be said: even the wealthy king will not be free, lest his spirit is awakened. Joy and freedom, which we are striving to experience, are only found within. In order to dwell in the light of truth and to free our own spirit, we human beings must experience ourselves. We must realise that this is a lonely road, and that the collective can't help us along.

Many people search for a fellowship of a spiritual nature, with spiritual goals. However, most of the time, there are only various forms of ego to be met there, who give each other well intended advice. This is not supposed to be a generalization - not all fellowships are bad, quite the contrary. But they shouldn't be chosen to lighten one's own load. They serve to complement one another, and to encourage mutual growth, but never as a remedy for one's own path of ascension. Only that which has been experienced within, and sensed in all its transitions, has been fully grasped by the human being and can be internalised!

The seeker will encounter his/her sufferings – and joys, too – in ever changing forms, thus being led towards a spiritual awakening. During this process, we will frequently experience moments of joining with the true, imbued spirit of truth.

This detachment, always lasting but a few seconds, affords the first insights in the true nature of the human being, which is eternal life.

The true awakening will firstly be perceptible as an inner conflict. We human beings are and were accustomed to identifying ourselves with the help of meaningful symbols as physical beings, owning a spirit. Our eyes, ears and feelings are and were our tools, which we used diligently, and of which we are very conscious. For long eras, we adorned our spirit with the help of these sensations, thus generating the experience of our given life. Whatever was seen, was also felt. Whatever was felt, was real.

We didn't know, and in many cases still don't know today, that the ability to see is dependant upon the brain. If the brain, the mind, is fed by the physical body – which is to say, if the brain only accepts as real whatever can be seen or otherwise sensed organically – we won't be able to see beyond space. We store all sensual perceptions in our spirit, just as our emotional issues flow into it, moulding our entire awareness. As man thinks, so he now lives.

If the seeker is now, with the help of books or personal life experiences, encountering a new, different option of reality, his/her spirit becomes involved, and the conflict begins. Because the spirit reacts quite perplexed to this new information. Thus, our quest begins by convincing our own spirit that there is more than the eye can see. There is an invisible world, which we have pushed into the beyond. Thus, we have been encouraging the spirit to be twofold, because this nourishes and enforces its limitations.

At this point, we recognise that we as human beings have truly become an expression of our own perception, and are aligning our whole life accordingly. The spirit draws everything it carries within itself and consequently, we are beings of our own choosing.

Now, if we awaken due to an unfamiliar yearning, we are confronted with these very facts. Our spiritual advancement has long since developed its own dynamics, and we don't realise that we have entered a prison, after having personally erected the enclosing walls, which are now separating us from the invisible.

Thus, we are now prompted to dissolve the old image of ourselves, along with all its consequences; and here, the second conflict is being created, because the spirit which man calls EGO defends itself.

At this point, our path is branching out once again. From fear of loss and of change, which again includes a loss, a new spirit awakens – a rather more „spiritual" spirit, which, nonetheless, once again very cunningly takes the old ego-spirit into consideration and provides it, albeit in a new way, with almost exactly the same thing as before, namely, with undivided attention. And so, mankind has walked down these paths of spiritual ego-renewal for centuries.

People wanted to grow, but they also wanted to stay in control of how this growth should occur.

If, after a long journey, and repeated hikes along the same paths, these facts are finally recognised, we awaken truly and factually: we are now ready to die. Now, we help our spirit to experience itself in a new way – and this means, we are now walking the Royal Road.

By definition, the Royal Road is the direct path towards a goal which is difficult to attain - although the word „direct" must, in his context, not be confused with „simple".

The Royal Road is the path that originates in God's Will. It leads the human being out of the causal entanglements (the temptations), thereby opening up a truly spiritual consciousness, which is the consciousness of truth.

The Royal Road is free of attractants; it requires undivided focus and is often uncomfortable. It never reinforces man's desire to rush spiritual growth.

The Royal Road is free of any religion and imparts neither enlightenment, nor any spiritual techniques. It is the path within, the path of factual spiritual transformation, and our only possibility to be led into our true spiritual home.

If this insight awakens inside the human being, the valley of tears is left behind and the person is free, experiencing a spiritual rebirth ... and may the Royal Road be travelled by each and every human being. Because God alone knows the way.

Man only sees what his/her concepts show him/her. Thus, we have been walking in circles for a long time, without making any real progress.

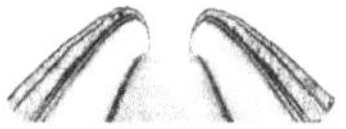

**„May spirit and soul be noble,
so that man can take
his place in creation.**

He is its crown.“

Andrea Regina Katharina InEssenz

The Crown of Creation

Actually, man is the crown of creation. He/she is and should be a being of sensitivity.

Thus, he/she is the desired link between spirit and matter. Uniting the ethereal of the beyond and the denseness of the material world within ourselves, we are able to survey both, to experience both at the same time. For that purpose, we are given a wonderful tool by God, which we have, however, misused.

God gave mankind the mind as the highest tool. With its help, we were supposed to control both worlds within ourselves - but for the progress of all creation, not for our own gains.

The mind is the tool of the dense material world, and the sensibility, the clairsentience, is the tool of the ethereal world. However, man used both tools in a completely different way than the Creator's Thought had wished.

Man used the mind for the purpose of analysis, to perceive things logically, and to scrutinize everything again and again. We have remodelled this tool, and it has become greater than man himself.

The mind is the head of the body. Sensibility is the head of the spirit.

As long as we nourish ourselves through the mind, we will live earthbound, because the mind itself is still too dense (condensed) to conquer space and time, even though it is already more ethereal than the dense physical body.

Man's clairsentience, his/her sensibility (not the emotions), has neither space nor time, and originates in the spiritual.

If we were equipped according to our nature, we would move in the progression of creation and grow naturally on the spiritual plane.

God be stowed this conjunction of spirit and matter inside a body-spirit only on the created being man.

Therefore, God's Plan was and is undivided: he created man as a link between the ethereal; invisible and holy, and the dense; material. He placed both worlds into the spirit and the soul of man, thus allowing us to accomplish the good as co-creators. Through man, the so-called dense, condensed world is supposed to become a permeable world of light again; and thus, God gave man a holy task.

However, we didn't accomplish this task. We divided the two worlds, rather than keeping them cohesive. And this was the so-called „fall"! Man began with the unique and sole task to saturate the dense with the ethereal. And with the free will, we probably received the highest power God provided – man was the appointed ruler of the earth. In due course, man truly did implement the saying „Subdue the earth". However, we did it in reverse; we did not do it to redeem matter, but have, by our conduct, bound the spirit more and more to the dense matter, thus creating the suffering of this world. Man was supposed to become a permeable vessel, open to the flow from the light sources, like an alternating electrical current. However, we interrupted this flow and caused congestion, which led to severe disruptions between spirit and matter. Illnesses, natural catastrophes and self-destruction were the result of this noncompliance.

All this could occur because man didn't use the mind as a tool to do good. Instead we submitted to the mind completely, and thereby chained ourselves to the dense. Thus, we created materialism, which is governing us, until we once again become a link between spirit and matter.

Because we ourselves tied the spirit to our feelings (not to our sensibility), we limited ourselves. Our abilities to perceive our surroundings were attached to the programmes of our mind. And thus, we created a wall around our sensations of the spiritual worlds, thereby interrupting the given, intended, natural flow. We isolated ourselves and thus, for millennia, have been experiencing ourselves in the mirror of our own creation.

God is, however, even more ethereal; he is the very source of the insubstantial, which has become so inaccessible to mankind. Man had superseded the access to the invisible, thus banning him-/herself from the experience of divine proximity. Therefore, in order to draw close to God, we first have to restore our natural sensibility.

When God forbade Adam and Eve to eat the fruits of the tree of knowledge, he made his ban into a testimony of his love. God knew that this fruit would bring fornication to the mind and disrupt the natural covenant. Because this fruit (the apple) would create the ego, which would constantly demand new insights. That's exactly what happened!

At this point, by tasting the fruit, the mind first experienced the possibility of bringing itself up, by continuously craving more knowledge, by greed. That's how the separation from the ethereal took place, which naturally resulted in the expulsion from God's Realm: paradise.

Thus, by self-inflicted fettering, began of the fall of creation, and bondage was invented.
But what and who is being fettered?

The answer is quite simple, since it originates in the results of mankind's deeds.

Through its inherent, creative power, every experienced thought instantly takes on a form according to the thought's ethereal contents, and thus continually remains connected to its creator. In this way, delicate threads are incessantly being woven, again and again returning to their creator, according to the principle of karmic law. However, before they do this, they outpour themselves into the vast cosmos, where they are drawn towards similar threads. Thus, they wander from one similar thought to the next. Once they have formed a big, ethereal elemental, they return to their creator by their formative line, there unloading themselves into all spiritual and physical bodies – even the soul's dwellings are thereby encumbered.

Once this process with its huge implications has become conscious, we will remember that we are destined for something higher. We will then begin to remove the threads we have spun spiritually, and replace them with the new, good thoughts we are now emanating. We need to know that this path is not an easy one, because our seed will be our harvest as well. But if our mind stays in the background during this process, and our ethereal sensibility can strengthen itself, we can pull the threads of light, the divine path, closer to our-selves, thus becoming more and more a link between spirit and matter. We are giving ourselves over as a vessel, which now gives and receives that which is pure, thereby moulding the earthly realm and the beyond into a unity.

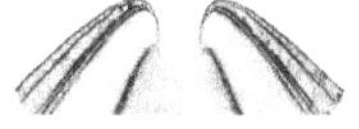

„Man can know nothing,
until he is wise.

His mind holds him
in the wheel of rebirth.

It needs to be diminished,
to let wisdom be."

Andrea Regina Katharina InEssenz

Separation from the Light

When man received his existence from God, the Forefather of all spiritual powers, a mighty tool was placed in his/her spiritual forms. He gave us a spiritual body, the mind, and crowned it to be the head of man. With this gift, mankind received the potential to control events occurring both on the inside, as well as on the outside.

Therefore, God the Creator gave us yet another tool: the free will. With this gift, man was able to choose. That which is facing the light is found in all spiritual realms, as well as that averting the light. The choice to obtain self-awareness either through God or without God was also made possible by the free will.

Due to the so called „spiritual impotence", which is the loss of self-awareness of the soul, man experienced an idiosyncratic condition. We lost our spiritual memory, suffering a „spiritual amnesia". The results were fatal, because, due to the consequential deafness and blindness, man needed to attempt to see and hear anew. We had no idea that we carried dual sensual realms within ourselves – the inner realm, facing the light, and the outward realm, turned towards matter (spiritual rigidity). Thus, we started to invent ourselves anew, outside of the divine will.

Because of the inclination to identify with the outer senses, mankind, throughout history, created a world full of suffering. Man's tendency towards the ignoble was growing incessantly, and we didn't even realise it. We created happiness according to shapes. We nourished ourselves with superfluous things, to experience a feeling of repletion. We copied our fellow human beings and steadily tried to reach some goal, which was constantly changing, even during the course of one lifetime. Thus, we lived ever faster and employed our life-powers to avoid feeling utterly helpless.

We might have sensed those processes, but due to the tool of our mind, to which we succumbed more and more, we lost all insight.

Without insight, we couldn't recognise the trap, but blundered right into it, even though nobody but we ourselves had set it up.

Throughout many epochs, the greater part of mankind behaved in that fashion, and accordingly, this creation Earth was provided with a government and with hierarchical systems, existing in total ignorance of the divine. Through this dense concentration of material spirits, man awakened the satanic spark he/she is carrying inside, as well as the realm within the Earth. Those souls who pledged themselves to darkness chose this as their own, and sole kingdom. These beings are being illuminated by the loving care of the Son of God. However, they don't realise it, because their spirit sees only that which is their own.

Because of all the suffering and the dark beings and powers arising from it, saturating Earth's soil, the Earth lost its divine balance and fell into disparity.

Thus, all kinds of shifts occurred, such as the shifts in climate, in animal populations, the minerals, the oceans and all other bodies of water.

But mankind remained oblivious to that which developed as well. The satanic deeds and words of mankind opened the locked gateway into Earth's „empire below", where the darkness nourished and multiplied its ancient power. In our tendency towards the ignoble, we ourselves permitted these beings to colonize the Earth. Thus, the purely demonic powers intermingled with divine man, and our destiny became (self-) determined.

And so it occurred that we separated ourselves from the divine truth by a deep gap, which was filled more and more with deeds and words of the human nature, until it reached an almost unredeemable size. This is the gap of the abyss. It needs to be cleaned out, because it contains mankind's seed, from which the harvest shall grow. This gap still exists, and while man separated from the light of truth and tasted mortality, the moribund multiplied. Sicknesses were created, which rose from the spirit of darkness and carried powers of self-destruction, which multiplied blazingly fast, and made the Earth into a self-destructing planet.

So, in this manner, life here is determined. Therefore all of us experience our lives in a continuous transformation between life and death. We cannot recognise ourselves as beings of peace to the extent in which this was born of itself. We fight; and are content when we reach a phase bearing fewer internal struggles.

Should we however, remember this, we can know one thing: inside of us we have an altar which serves to honour God. This altar is the godly atom, which allows us to sense clairvoyant. Is our sensitivity kind, loving, caring, mindful and ompassionate, reception is the answer from paradise. Thus there are moments in which we can feel the presence of God intensively; as so often happens in times of deepest sorrow and greatest joy!

These sensations, which often last mere seconds, constitute the true life of the soul, as the purely spiritual beings in paradise experience it continuously. Here we may now receive the key which opens the gate enabling us to leave helplessness and enter into the light of veracity.

When the simple, highly spiritual and pure souls bow to humanity, they place the simple form of living into the human spirit: the spiritual good of eternal love. They awaken the godly powers sleeping in the background and help us to create ourselves anew, so that we make the wish to love God above all else our own personal first commandment – not by means of learning methods, nor through acquisition by hard work: instead, the pure souls give this to their weaker spiritual brethren out of the grace of unselfish love. It awakens our natural heritage to remember the Father and let the Child-Father relationship to God ascend.

The Erroneous Paths of Personal Empowerment

The majority of seekers, but also those who lead their lives without conscious change are caught up in a serious mistake which causes them to wander aimlessly.

It is not God's task to wait and hope for a person to believe in him and love him unconditionally. God's messengers also need not incarnate themselves era after era in order to admonish and lead us out of our self-inflicted ruination. It is God's pure love to the human being which constantly instigates this valuable process and grants the help needed time and time again.

The biggest confusion concerning the character of God stems from the churches. Serious and assiduous ministers reach out to the earthly people, to the matter-of-fact persons, in order to convert and convince them to join the church. This „act of warning" and well-meaning work of promoting peace often causes the faithful to become introverted and feel as though they are being forced to do good superficially: for example through compulsory prayer or the wish to no longer feel badly about themselves. This belief is imposed upon people from the outside and the true godly experience is lost. So much misuse can thereby happen to the faithful – as well as among those who minister to their God-seeking charges. True and honest faith would never include such misuse and dependency.

Denominational creeds particularly accept God-seeking persons. Due to deeply ingrained awareness of personal failings, helplessness and the feeling of being short-lived and without directional orientation, people are only too eager to be led. In this feeling of being uplifted they sense an homage to God; a sort of thankfulness from God for obedience. They feel a certain union with God. Occasionally the thought of this causes them to experience a sort of „holy trembling," evoking a sense of blessedness which they happily enjoy.

When Jesus spoke of the Pharisees he meant that people of faith do not always perform their deeds or take that which they speak from the same source. They feel better about themselves because they believe in something and pray. However, if prayer does not come from the soul, it is nothing other than hollow words and serves only the self-satisfactory feeling of having done something good.

Let it be said that this does not apply to all people. True seekers of God and true ministers can also be found among them. „By their fruits shall ye know them," as they do not leave a trail of smoke behind nor smile to hide their discontent. They are kind and their souls speak of God. Spiritual arrogance should, however, not be found in seekers and the faithful. If prayer consists only of demands and if darker practices still occur in religions; it would be better to look for another pastime.

It is therefore advisable for everyone to sincerely seek God and earnestly try to stand before Him as a true worshipper. As soon as we enter the ethereal non-corporeal world; which happens upon physical death; all we may have hidden falls away and we stand before God in the face of our own spiritual condition.

This demonstrates that in all ways a person can choose to be near God, honesty, sincerity and authenticity are the absolute benchmark for a life in the light of truth. If this is recognised and practised, one then finds him-/herself on the Royal Road leading to the spiritual home.

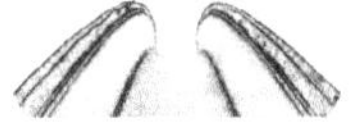

Occult Training

Is it advisable to support progress through occult training? We can answer this with a resounding „no!". All methods purporting to lead us into the so-called areas of clairvoyance, clairaudience or other heightened senses of awareness are hindrances of natural, spiritual growth and the dissolution of the karma chain clouding true spiritual development. What is taught with these techniques is rather a type of magic which is at best harmless and at worst, pulls us down into completely impure regions.

Even those teachers who allegedly pick up students where they find themselves in spirituality at the moment are overreaching the goal. The students see and hear only the level which they attract through their own spirit. Howsoever they behave in this earthly, material form; how they treat fellow humans, how free their emotional range may be, how humble their heart – these are all threads, defining the webs spun by the students in the invisible regions.

Often are the received messages conveyed by so-called earthbound souls which cling to LIFE, because they do not recognise the ascent into the light. At best a somewhat spiritually elevated entity arrives and leads the students venturing into these areas back to their earthly lives through well-meaning suggestions.

A trained clairvoyant or clairaudient often finds him-/herself at a misleading level through occult training. Supposedly the student finds the Exalted and the Pure here – and follows these good instructions – but these are often disguises hiding the other side.

We dare not forget that people have vivid imaginations which spring from their wishes and hopes. In this manner, the student of the occult can actually create an ambience in which he/she can „hear" and „see." This so-called talent, though, has been drawn in and released by others and usually stands upon an unhealthy and unclean foundation.

Thus the „seer" cannot discern where the border between truth and suggestion lies. He/

she is on thin ice which can break at any time. The student also forms easily the compulsion to act in the same manner in earthly life, in order to progress more rapidly.

A person who has neither been called nor led by the comportment of an upright spirit and yet enters these depths is like a diver who ventures to undergo a dive without compressed air and other necessary diving equipment. Such an individual would be exposed to great danger by sinking into depths in which a natural breath is insufficient. These persons have ventured forth into an element whose primal form is unknown to them. Being not adapted to it, its primal laws will affect them.

The difference between a student of the occult and a diver is as follows: a diver notices quite quickly that he/she is diving without compressed air. The occult student, however, believes to be safe and secure. His/her spirit is enraptured at being able to hear and see far beyond the natural ears and eyes. Due to ignorance, the student is unable to see the snares and so becomes further and further enmeshed into the supposed images and messages.

However, there are also those with a true calling among the „seers." These individuals know through their own maturity that they must not encourage the inexperienced seeker to practice what they do and thereby venture into unknown waters. These people have become observers and listeners of the higher ethereal beings in order to help the earthly students with unresolved issues or situations by recognising the connections and causes. These appointees are secure and can draw Good to Earth through higher beings. They are careful and recognise the masked enemy immediately, because their souls are connected in maturity to the truth.

Should we encounter a teacher of occult studies, it is best to remain at a distance and wait until our own behaviour brings our soul to maturity in order to be able to lift the curtains still hiding the Exalted; for it is easy to advance into the levels of magic, as these wait for eager, unwary souls in order to enrich themselves upon them. States of purity cannot be reached through occult teachings for experimentation; but rather only by uplifting the true, internal ethics with a permanant eye towards the purity of light.

If we decide to embark upon the path to the realm of God via pure intention, we first think of our own souls. We behave with kindness towards ourselves, as well as towards other people. Also, we have no ambitions to press on at all costs, having recognised that our own eyes and ears are dulled by our own spiritual attitude.

Thus, we begin to clean our own spiritual attitude, until we are able to move between all intermediary levels. This means that before we can see into the higher worlds, we must prove ourselves – we must transform our personal character traits back to the Pure and the Good. This is necessary in order not to be held in the levels corresponding to our spirit. Otherwise we would meander into great misfortune, which is often not at first apparent, but will certainly appear later. However, should we travel the healthy path and firstly allow ourselves to gradually clear away all that is barring the way to the higher domain of the spiritual world, the boundary becomes thinner and thinner and then we are natural seers – moving like fish through familiar waters – without being exposed to the danger of being eaten by sharks. This is the only sure way.

What remains unrecognised in occult teaching – and what a teacher rarely tells the students – is that the latter decide to undergo these studies of clairvoyance and clairaudience out of free will. The student encourages and receives images, visions and messages; thereby changing the soul-spirit and personal perception greatly. Since it is seldom pure beings that thus come down to the students, they experience an encounter from the intermediary realms. This means they receive neither healing, nor do they progress. It is merely a satisfaction for the lesser human spirit.

Because the student has embarked on this road voluntarily, no help can come from the higher world. This person remains without protection, because – in the belief of having done the right thing – no further, correctional access is possible due to the determination of free will. Here we can see just how dangerous this road is.

There are also a number of teachers who, with the help of ayahuasca (or other hallucinogenic agents) attempt to sink themselves into states of trance, which expand consciousness and there-by supposedly lift the veils which have settled over the spirit and soul. These seers possess no maturity, as they adopt substances in order to promote growth. Indigenous peoples have used these substances to bring healing to the Earth. During the course of the further evolution of man, however, the use of these hallucinogenic agents has become an attempt to free oneself from one's own life. Here we can say, this is NOT the Will of God.

In closing this chapter, a word of summarisation and insight. All this does not mean that the area of the ethereal world should remain untouched and unexplored in earthly life!

The right time will come to the inwardly matured, so that they can move securely within the invisible realms which will reveal themselves to their sprits slowly but surely in order to unite Heaven and Earth. These individuals will always be accompanied, well-protected and will never succumb to the siren call of occult teachings.

The Holy Power of Healing
Healing magnetism

Healing magnetism is the strength of the human vessel. It is the stream of high healing powers which need man as their tool to free the Earth of illness and various ailments.

This is not about the large number of people who – with average „energy emission" and many words – try to show the seeker the way und thereby have given themselves permission as healers to deal with invisible powers.

The healer who has been called by God experiences him-/herself as the vessel of the complete body. Such a healer carries a pure spirit and his/her earthly body is the flowing healing magnetism which comes from the higher realms into the material world. These „magnetopaths" can be found all over the Earth. They are all recognisable by the same behaviour and course of action. They love God above all things, they promise no miracles and they do not speak of wonders which they have performed. They are the quiet – yet intense – messengers of pure love and every individual who can find them in the huge self-proclaimed „spiritual" world is a fortunate spirit.

Healing magnetism is the power of Christ. This light-power, which brings blessings, holds within itself all the spiritual virtues which stem from the perfect Spirit of God.

The person who carries them has gone through a long spiritual road and has dissolved all his/her vices. His/her soul is free in the Light of God and can thereby absorb the true currents of God and deposit these into creation. True, strong healing power cannot be learned. It is an inherent gift which has identified the individual talented with it as an appointee.

Magnetopaths do not have an easy task here on Earth, when they have been appointed by God, because they speak a different tongue. They do not flaunt their talents, nor are there any posters displaying their names.

The seeker truly looking to return to God should, however, find these people. They are the real pillars for a true ascent into the light.

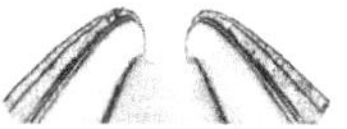

„The Love of God is
the only constant
from the beginning until the
end of all days and
moves into eternity.“

Andrea Regina Katharina InEssenz

It is opened

When we speak here of gateways, these are not synonymous with those which a person can access by traditional means in order to broaden one's horizons or to enter spiritual realms intrusively, so as to „sweeten" his or her own path.

Now the time of truth has arrived, as it is already 12 o´clock for mankind. The time to exploit fully the game of self-determination is now coming to an end. All people who have been elevated to bring the true word to Earth and its inhabitants and to awaken the eternal powers within them are now called to walk the great Royal Road. They are also called to refine it for those who are to follow and enter this road as well; from now on in this time.

You, the chosen, who are already connected to the spiritual world, have within you a call to deliver. You should declare your affiliation with God and speak the just, godly word. You should turn to the powers of the Eternal exclusively and not visit any intermediary realms with your granted gifts. You have already been partially relieved of the burden of the cross within you; and that was not done in order for you to place yourselves in the word. You should carry God's Word as a living light into the world, thereby bringing forth the new out of the old.

These talents have been granted you solely from this law, which God Himself created: uncondition-al Love of God, which carries over to your fellow man. These talents do not belong to you. You have received them merely as a loan and must renew yourselves before you can say, „I am soul and I have a gift." And so will only those of you be led to the truth, who have recognised that you have been sent by God, who always was and always shall be – in order to bring Him nearer to humanity; free of human ideas.

The great purification has already begun. If we look around we can see the effects clearly. God wants to have the inhabitants of Earth; but not the headstrong, who draw upon themselves in order to be elevated.

Those of us who follow the Word of God, beyond all scriptures, will build the new realm, be blessed and guided. The strength of exalted love will flow into all of us who are true and honest and live the Divine. Together we will bring good to the Earth and Lucifer's entourage will be demolished by the power of salvation. We will free the Earth of all egotistical self-declared authority and the results thereof. We shall sit at a richly prepared table at the right Hand of God, taste an abundant feast and will be anointed with oil.

During the time of the persecution of Christians and the times of the betrayal against God's Son Jesus Christ there were – even as there are today – people who did not allow themselves to be influenced by this and professed their belief in God and his Son. Even when they were betrayed and sentenced to death, they remained true. Up through time until today, this discipleship has been renewed time and time again. Even today the loyal servants of the „Exalted Love" exist. It was they who laid the good powers into Creation, so that others might follow them. There are, however, still many errors on Earth and the harvest arising out of the centuries is a great drought in the hearts of man.

Nonetheless there is a joyful message – Lucifer is already BOUND. His powers hardly renew themselves and the harvest of his deeds – through himself and his followers – are that which needs to be redeemed through avowal to God and commitment to Him. Lucifer's power is demolished and those who still are with him are the last followers of his earthly means of expression. The so-called „dark sides" of humanity are also stricken and more debilitated than in centuries past; for the light is now on Earth. It has found its way into Creation and offers itself equally to all beings. It will penetrate the ruthless until they dissolve into shadows and either withdraw themselves or ascend to God.

During the time of persecution of Christians and the arrival of Jesus on the Earth, it was much more difficult for people to lean on God, as the dark enemy was powerful and killed many believers.

Today humanity can truly rise more easily, for only the last remaining cohorts remain, who have absorbed shadows through Lucifer.

Out of the Love of God a river of light – a current of unimaginable, indescribable strength – will flow into all willing and true seekers. Courage will seethe up within you and become a glowing flame which stretches toward all shadows and slings its sparks into all that it encounters. This grace is with you – all of you who respect and honour God. Be therefore careful of what you speak, and to whom you turn for help.

The ascent is only about the entrance into the realm of God. Those who avoid His name today will retain the crosses which they bear.

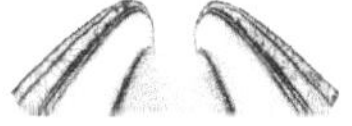

**„Man can never know peace,
if he ignores godly law.**

**To observe it is the
essence of healing."**

Andrea Regina Katharina InEssenz

The Adjustment to True Peace

There is a primal law of creation which has been inducted into us. It is the primal divine truth to live through creation in respect and honesty. However, due to the fact that humanity has wrapped itself in a shell consisting of words and experiences which have varied spiritual forms and light structures, even the link to God and the primal essence is an abstraction, a wrapping. Mankind was separated from its natural essence.

We are, however fashioned from spirit, which is intangible, in order to become tangible beings, who through stirring and compensatory actions prove themselves to be carriers of the godly shafts of light. The intangible primal law created perfect spiritual beings and sent them out into diverse areas after the evolution of all floral and mineral realms was completed.

We as beings of coarse material were given lasting access to the spiritual realm. Today we

tend to call this connection intuition, „gut feeling"
or abdominal brain.

There is, however an error present in this.
The abdominal brain is connected to the intellect
and the field of emotional information. It carries
the good and the bad, as well as the true and the
untrue. The abdominal brain has the purpose of
differentiating between the one and the other, so
that it can in retrospect, without intellectual experience, make decisions. Because we need access
to distinctiveness, however, which we cannot find
here, we often find ourselves caught in a feeling of
„perhaps" and are helpless.

We have become beings led by the mind. This
is situated in our forebrain of the human being.
All programming of every period and every form
is recorded here. This is accomplished through
thought forms which in turn parcel themselves
out and take up residence in the various centres
(energy centres) and soul domiciles – like an engra-
ving. Here is where we form the greater portion of
our personalities. If this part of the brain is over-
taxed, this results in many patterns of disease;
i.e. of psychological, physical or emotional nature.

The forebrain has become the control centre of human life and bears the title of all programmes: MAN, THY WILL BE DONE.

If none of this flood of information is drained, anyone can see that spiritual release from the past is impossible. The only primal error lies here when we give this process a name. Therefore, it is we alone who hold ourselves back. We taper ourselves down to our intellect and do all we can to improve it. We fail to recognise that it carries nothing other than that which has been fed into it, for only imaginary knowledge, imaginary peace exists here.

If the „food" happened to be an enlightening form of thought, this centre can recover somewhat. The forebrain needs relief and finds it in sleep. Then it can relieve itself and drain off some of that which we have given it as a body of thought. The hindbrain can finally come into play now. Employing dreams and the unconsciousness which sets in upon sleep, it transforms disturbing forms of thought, which it has already prepared for removal, into forms containing more light, so that the intellect and deposited thought can modify themselves beneficially. This is why sleep is so important for us. It empties our reservoir of information, which brings relief to our brain cells.

The hindbrain, however, neither sleeps nor rests. It receives godly wisdom and healing power to enable a life in godly order permanently from the spiritual realm by means of the chain of energy. The intellect, however, slows down these emanations, thereby autonomously cutting off human nature from the divine completely.

The programmes „Sight", „Hearing", „Feeling" – and the tendency of wanting to understand and control everything through them – are the walls which have been erected between spirit and matter. Only a single individual can tear them down by being prepared to let the forebrain rest.

However, the road of ascension, which at the present time is being travelled by so many seek-ers, is now also subject to the same pattern. The seekers try to reach the hindbrain by various types of implementation: meditation and other practices which promise to bring light. In this manner we try desperately to circumvent our programmes and do not recognise that this is impossible. We can only achieve the adjustment we need through our own action.

We must relax completely into the human beings we are: not wanting to understand or see – ideally, to be blind and deaf – and simply let the programmes discharge themselves in us. We must learn not to flee before them or overwrite them (re-programme anew). Only in this way can the peace-bringing light beams of truth reach us. That cannot be achieved through the aid of other people, trainers or teachers, but through our own spirits which can then liberate themselves.

All images, all ideas of how something functions must be erased! Our own sense of purpose must be erased. Jesus illustrated with his words how that is accomplished: through behaviour pleasing to God – „Lord, thy will be done."

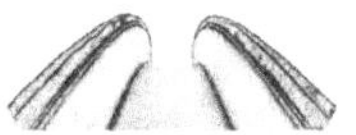

Further Guidelines

The souls and human spirits of all people now incarnated on Earth are still integrated in the information levels of the causal world. We are all governed by the longings of the soul and thereby experience a craving which would like to be satisfied by the healing powers of the spiritual level.

During the course of Earth's eras many people have undergone paths of cleansing in order to free themselves from the bondage of the eternal cycle. This is a good undertaking, as Lucifer's destructive force was thereby bound.

For better comprehension of this: Lucifer is eternal. He stems from the realm of the divine-Substance. He is an intimate brother of Christ. The essential-divine-cognisance was formed from Christ: Jesus. Out of Lucifer, a being was formed, who was – according to the Will of God – supposed to have revealed divine order to all Creation. Lucifer was given the assignment of fostering spiritual beings in their development and to promote with the love of the divine-unsubstantiate (God's Love) all virtues leading to godly order.

This mission, however, was not fulfilled by Lucifer's spirituality. And so began the first disarray in the spiritual realm. He introduced the unauthorised principle of temptation and seduced the immature spirit of the tangible beings to commit character deeds of egoism and self-love. These sowed destructive seeds and attracted all spirits, who were still too immature to recognise what was transpiring – in other words, all of humanity.

Lucifer is invulnerable. He is in the eternal realm, although Satan, the being of temptation is tangible along with his entire entourage and is subject to change through honourable powers. Whoever can comprehend this with his/her present level of consciousness will recognise that everything comprising a single person has not yet liberated the godliness within.

This deliverance can only occur when the spirit together with the mind is developed as a spiritual, conscious being. This spirit is weary of temptation and begins to dissolve those patterns within itself by turning towards the pure Good.

God is bodiless and is the eternal power from which everything possessing no self-will originated. This power has no benchmark standard. It can neither escalate nor plummet. It can neither judge nor favour. It remains constant and stable. All that comes from it serves the good is the good.

And so it can be said that no religion should worship this power, because it needs neither rituals nor rules. It is freely available and can only be realised when an individual spirit is open to it. For this reason we must free ourselves from God as the being, who gives something, demands something and takes something. God is an eternal divine order, whose expressiveness cannot be sufficiently encompassed – not even by the word love. When a spiritual being, a person who advances him-/herself spiritually towards the good experiences God, he/she does not experience a being. We rather experience the unsubstantiate divinity, which reveals itself once we have turned in that direction and have dismissed Satan from within.

In this manner the new God-Consciousness can awaken with all blessings and spiritual medicine. The name „God" should be renewed and recognised in all that is. We now know what is meant when we are told that we are godly. Only when we let go of our intellect will we recognise the godly principle and simply live – that is all there is to do.

May mankind become simple, in order to become wise.

Prophecies of Seers
Possible Fulfilment

The most diverse of prophets from all eras left behind prophecies of the so-called „Day of Judgment". They spoke of a great star, a particular comet which – at the proper hour – will empty itself over the Earth and darkness lasting several days is its legacy. The number of people who long for the fulfilment of this prophecy grows daily. However, it remains unclear what sort of cataclysm this comet will bring.

It is a star (comet) which – spiritually speaking – is full of pure power and surrounded by material substance. This is at any rate the historical tradition. The comet's radiation brings such earthquakes and great world catastrophes as humanity has never known. The Father of all Creation released this star out of the pure spiritual realms and sent it on its way. It will appear at the appointed time and bring enlightenment to those people who have shown themselves to be faithful to the core of their souls. This procedure was without doubt formulated millennia ago, and now great world changes are upon us and the prophecies can be fulfilled. What exactly this will entail is unknown. All that can be said is that it will take years before the star's rays will have freed the Earth from all suffering. Thereafter the Earth will have become that spirit which, out of the Will of God, created the planet which we humans have so debased.

Every true believer can be consoled and steeped in rising joy, for if that which the seers described and which we can already perceive when we all observe creation and its character truly happens, so let the following be acknowledged: we may all pray that the star of renewal comes to mankind. The appointed hour will soon arrive.

What all of us are experiencing on Earth is the harvest of a seed which was sown without the streaming divine atom. It is impudent to believe that man actually has power. Mankind is the most helpless species in all creation. Without our forms and images we are lost in space, as we cannot depend on anything but our own self-created mortality.

Know this: no human being who trusts God and places himself into God's Hands will ever be inflicted with suffering.

**„Whoever grants healing
must be refined in spirit.**

**He should know his soul and
love God beyond measure.“**

Andrea Regina Katharina InEssenz

The Essence of all Words

Man can only exist through Divine-Unsubstantiate. This created all life in every form of existence. The soul and spirit of man are spiritual essential forces. Together they comprise the Creation-Child of God. By means of incarnation, a further created being arose: the human being.

Our bodies are provided for by heavenly power and they receive this through the spirit and soul.

Thus arose a new form of existence – the eternal combined with the perishable: spirit, soul, body. This trinity requires each of these three components. They all experience the same thing, which flows from word, deed and thought.

The human being; the personality-being is favoured here, as we have many opportunities of attenuating ourselves. Through contact with the material we have created a field of illusion. The spirit is woven into this field and made part of it, so that the mind is formed and carries all the information which flows into it.

The soul cannot soothe itself. It receives all the information undiluted and relentlessly. Because it has also lost the spirit to the human being, it suffers greatly. This was not planned. God's idea differed from that which now rules the world.

Here follows a sober explanation of correct action in order to become a spiritual, conscious being. All seekers should know:
You should not try to develop your own identity by seeking contact with your soul in order to live a better life; out of the hope that you will obtain health and peace through the strength of the soul. On the one hand it is commendable to refine the connection of the soul to man, but the intention is - for the most part - of personal nature. The motive consists of gaining something for oneself.

But here, the seeker is forgetting one thing. We live through the soul and it carries our forms of thought within itself. All of our actions must be concentrated around granting the soul peace, removing barriers from the soul, bringing it nearer to God's presence, relieving it from pain – the pain which comes from the spiritually unconscious attitude of the human being in general.

This we must sense within ourselves, because it is we who have pulled the soul down and estranged the spirit. It is therefore our duty to care for the soul and place EGO in the background.

To all healers and all people employed in healing on Earth the following must be said:
All of our talents should serve the purpose of reminding our fellow human beings that the soul and spirit should be ennobled through good thoughts, good words and good works. All healing emanations, all knowledge was granted us in order to awaken this godly aspect in our personalities. All healing powers should be employed to free the spirit, which has been pulled down, from all thoughts of self-empowerment. The highest duty of the healer should be to praise the divine and to consider self as being insignificant. It is not a question of religion.

God the Father, Christ the Son and the Holy Spirit as all-inclusive expressional power of the holy trinity exist together as creational power. No entity other than his should be worshipped or called upon. We are all children of this power and were entrusted with a soul and spirit, which we should treat with loving care.

This is our duty:

First we must recognise that no-one should give or take for personal reasons. This includes all people, whether those employed in healing capacities, as well as seekers. All of us should be conscious of the fact that the point is always to praise the divine.

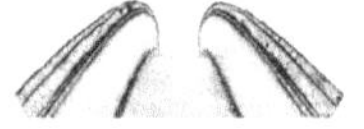

93

The Ascent to Mount Carmel

According to St. John of the Cross; described and interpreted by Andrea Regina Katharina InEssenz

To the right of the path, those people can be recognised who do not keep a connection to God in their minds. Rather, they concentrate on the material and their own needs.

To the left of the path are those people who have set out on their way and move spiritually, but do not have God as a goal. If one observes the signs carefully, it is recognisable that this path leads not to the top of the mountain, but rather into nothingness.

Then there are the half-hearted, who allow themselves to be impressed by the path they are travelling, often stand still and do not progress earnestly enough.

All three of the groups described here find them-selves under a dark cloud representing the „Dark Night of the Soul." Every person who wishes to reach the mountaintop must pass through here.

In the middle, the soul which is courageous e-nough to go through the „Dark Night" can be seen. It advances towards God ... it is the way of the soul and the individual should climb with it and not deter the soul through his/her own behaviour.

Many souls have set out on the path of virtue, yet as soon as people are then led by God into the „Dark Night," where they may experience purification and godly unity, many cannot come to terms with this situation, because they have not recollected their souls and have allowed themselves to be led by their emotions.

And so they remain behind, helpless, in this Night. They suffer spiritual crises or turn back to a life in a pond, without recalling God. Most people lack a „guide" (God), who can lead them to the mountaintop and can grasp the „Dark Night." There are countless souls being held back from the guiding hand of God by man, so it is no wonder that humanity has made no pro-gress towards its deliverance into peace.

Let it be said and recognised here:
Without godly guidance there can be no freedom for the soul and mankind remains caught in the cycle of reincarnation. Without God, a spiritual life and spiritual understanding are impossible. Everything which we experience without God is occult and does not lead us back into eternal love. We should simply love God without using Him or demanding anything from Him.

Afterword

The quest for redemption has entered human awareness and therefore innumerable people have set out to search for it. They have created many practices, relics and writings in order to glean a possible glimmer of truth and light. Most go the way of so-called ascent following the parameters set by their brothers and sisters, without realising that these predecessors are often still seekers themselves, whose calling often stems from their own cry. This results in the experience that many paths lead back into the cycle of reincarnation and are – at best – simply assistance for moderate progress.

If we are serious abut coming closer to the truth and BECOMING the truth, we must first purge everything we have learned or read. We must brush aside our own personality and begin – completely naïve and simple – to allow ourselves to be restructured anew. We must confront the new like a child, completely harmless and without accessing the past. Imagining riding a bicycle for the first time; possibly without knowing how to do it; can facilitate this process.

This appears simple, yet it is the most difficult hurdle for humanity today. Purging the personal „library" of acquired knowledge seems well nigh impossible; accustomed as we are to interlinking all that we know – the good with the bad in all variations.

A serious search is almost unachievable for mankind, as this leads to regions which demand that everything situated outside of godly truth must be erased. With this in mind we began to embellish our search. The modern „spiritual fun-fair" demonstrates the diversity of ideas inherent in the desperate human mind – first and foremost the beloved light, which is freely obtainable everywhere.

The fact that everything is light – including the so-called karma-filled light – seems to have slipped by the ever faster forward moving mankind. None of the „awakened" seem to realise that vanity and competition have seeped into the search. Everyone speaks of enlightenment and redemption, but few refer thereby to the relationship of these qualities to God and Christ. Even Jesus is used today to invoke religious rapture and hardly anyone is quiet, peaceful and humble; let alone full of deep love of God.

To absorb consciousness of the Father of all Creation and let it grow to maturity means more than sublime feelings and the oh, so highly regarded knowledge which we mention so grandly.

Man is neither master, nor in possession of any such characteristics. The human race is simply a thought of God, which was intended to spread, thereby promoting beauty and truth. When we observe this world and the so-called ascent of man, we hear the words, „soul," „enlightenment" and „expanded consciousness" all too often. These are, however, merely terms and produce spiritual elevation for a few seconds at most – without duration. As long as we are unconcerned about entering into the heavenly realm, being a source of joy for our Creator through our own good actions, we shall only progress intellectually until our minds weaken and require new nourishment.

May the truth manifest itself and encompass mankind.

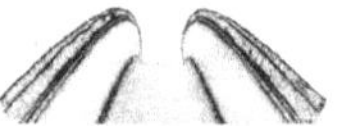

„The Wisdom of God
is the breath which sustains you.
The knowledge of mankind
is the faltering breath.

If you seek insights,
so begin here.

You live because you are wanted
and eternally loved,
not because you keep yourself alive.

It is your assignment to say
THANK YOU
and to let all the ignoble be elevated
by the Creator of all Life."

Andrea Regina Katharina InEssenz

About the Author

Andrea Regina Katharina InEssenz is an original Christian mystic and lives secluded from society in a small town in Germany.

Since her revival experience she spiritualises in the flesh something bestowed upon very few people. She brings the purest light to Earth and has insight into the highest dimensions of consciousness. Not only did her inner path change through this higher transformation, but her outer environment lost importance and security as well.

Devotion to godly power was and is the only possibility of existence. The „Holy Fire" burns within her and has illuminated her soul. Her path liberates from all religions, all forms of evaluation, all polarities and dualities which people carry within themselves. Her charisma serves world peace and facilitates experiencing God.

Encounters with Andrea

The great love of God flows through Andrea's body into the outside world and thereby helps all beings; human and animal alike; to attain personal transformation. The proximity of God is the vehicle which through the presence - the pure being of Andrea - is given.

The path of incarnation into human nature placed a veil over free, spiritual strength and caused forgetfulness of that which is TRUE. Thereby a new spiritual world arose - the visible world, which everyman perceives and helps to shape. This is, however, merely a copy of the impermeable spirit and needs to be cleansed, clarified and to return to the pure source. This is the longing of mankind.

Andrea's great mission is to let us experience our own light again. This happens through Christ and God Himself, both of whom manifest themselves through the mere presence of Andrea.

Her existence here on Earth is an act of grace and a gift to all humanity.

The only wish Andrea Regina Katharina InEssenz has is:

„May a healthy spiritual attitude and intense love of God be given to all people. It is quite easy to love God, as He demands nothing …
He only wishes to be loved."

You can find contact, videos and
the possibility of an encounter with
Andrea Regina Katharina InEssenz
on her website:
www.andrea-inessenz.de